SELECTED POEMS

MICHAEL HOFMANN

SELECTED POEMS

FARRAR STRAUS GIROUX

NEW YORK

Farrar, Straus and Giroux
18 West 18th Street, New York 10011

Originally published in 2008 by Faber and Faber Limited, Great Britain
Published in the United States by Farrar, Straus and Giroux
First American edition, 2009

Grateful acknowledgment is made to the editors of the following
publications, where some of the new poems first appeared: Granta (100),
London Review of Books, Ploughshares, Poetry, and The Times Literary Supplement.

Library of Congress Cataloging-in-Publication Data
Hofmann, Michael, 1957, Aug. 25–
    [Poems. Selections]
    Selected poems / Michael Hofmann.— 1st American ed.
        p. cm.
    ISBN-13: 978-0-374-25882-5 (alk. paper)
    ISBN-10: 0-374-25882-1 (alk. paper)
    I. Title.

PR6058.0345A6 2009
821'.914—dc22

                                            2008048144

Design and composition by Quemadura

www.fsgbooks.com

1 3 5 7 9 10 8 6 4 2

FOR JAMES LASDUN AND PIA DAVIS

Contents

FROM

NIGHTS IN THE IRON HOTEL

(1983)

White Noise 3

Pavement Artistes 5

Gruppenbild ohne Dame 6

Family Holidays 7

The Magic of Mantovani 8

Boys' Own 10

Lord B. and Others 12

By Forced Marches 13

l'an trentiesme de son eage 14

Shapes of Things 16

Furth i. Wald 17

On Fanø 19

Fates of the Expressionists 20

Nights in the Iron Hotel 21

Body Heat 22

FROM

ACRIMONY

(1986)

Ancient Evenings 25

On the Margins 26

Changes 28

Aerial Perspective 29

A Floating City 30

A Brief Occupation 32

Entr'acte 33

Nighthawks 34

From Kensal Rise to Heaven 36

Open House 39

This Sporting Death 40

Kif 42

Disturbances 43

Between Bed and Wastepaper Basket 45

Campaign Fever 47

Day of Reckoning 49

The Machine That Cried 50

My Father's House Has Many Mansions 52

Bärli 54

Lighting Out 55

Vortex 56

Withdrawn from Circulation 58

Giro Account 60

Catechism 62

My Father at Fifty 63

Author, Author 65

Fine Adjustments 69

Old Firm 71

FROM
CORONA, CORONA
(1993)

Lament for Crassus 75

The Late Richard Dadd, 1817–1886 77

Max Beckmann: 1915 79

Kurt Schwitters in Lakeland 81

Marvin Gaye 83

Sally 84

Freebird 85

Up in the Air 87

Wheels 89

Schönlaterngasse 91

Dean Point 92

The Day After 93

From A to B and Back Again 94

Days of 1987 95

Pastorale 96

On the Beach at Thorpeness 97

Postcard from Cuernavaca 98

Las Casas 100

Progreso 102

Sunday in Puebla 103

Aerogrammes, 1—5 105

Guanajuato Two Times 106

FROM

APPROXIMATELY NOWHERE

(1999)

For Gert Hofmann, died 1 July 1993 111

What Happens 112

Directions 113

Last Walk 114

Endstation, Erding 116

Zirbelstrasse 118

Still Life 120

de passage 122

Cheltenham 123

Metempsychosis 125

Essex 126

Fidelity 127

Ingerlund 129

Parerga 130

Vecchi Versi 131

Intimations of Immortality 132

Rimbaud on the Hudson 134

Scylla and Minos 135

Gone 138

Vagary 139

June 140

Megrim 141

Near Hunstanton 142

Seele im Raum 143

XXXX 145

Malvern Road 147

Lewis Hollow Road 150

Fairy Tale 152

Gomorrah 154

Night Train 156

Litany 158

NEW POEMS

Motet 163

Broken Nights 164

Hudson Ride 167

Idyll 169

Poem 171

End of the Pier Show 172

November 176

FROM

NIGHTS IN THE IRON HOTEL

(1983)

White Noise

It blows your mind,

the radio, or whatever piece of sonic equipment
you keep along with the single white rose
and the spiked mirror in your monochrome room . . .
I've seen it through the open door sometimes.

You hoover twice a week, and in my eyes
that amounts to a passion for cleanliness.
The vacuum, its pre-war drone in the corridor.
Thin and snub-nosed, a gas-mask on a stick.

Your reveille is at six: you go downstairs
for a glass of water with your vitamin pills.
Then back to your room, and your light stays on
till late.—What do you do to kill the time?

. . . Trailing cigarette smoke and suspicion,
you prowl through the house, accident-prone
and painfully thin in your sepulchral clothes.
Reality filters through your tinted spectacles.

And in the afternoon, your looped-tape excesses:
a couple of pop standards in your repertoire,
the demonstration piece for synthesizer,
and that thrilling concerto for nose-flute . . .

Two floors away, I can still hear the storm.
The jungle and the platitudes of sentiment
battle it out with technology, sweep you
into a corner of your room, delirious, trembling,

a pile of leaves.

Pavement Artistes

AFTER E. L. KIRCHNER

His women are birds of paradise, cocottes:
stiletto-heeled, smoking, dressed to kill.
They wear veils to cage the savagery

of their features. Like the motherly pelican,
they are plucked bare—except their hats,
which are feathered and tipped like arrows.

They live together on a green traffic island.
Berlin Zoologischer Garten—*tristes tropiques*!
The station clock measures their allurements.

Their control of outlying stairways and arches
is ensured by their human architecture.
The gothic swoop of shoulder, waist and hip.

For men, they are something of a touchstone,
distinguishing them into the two categories
of policeman and clown . . . You can see both types

strolling down the boulevard, bowler-hatted
and terrified of shadows—sometimes testing
the street's temperature with a long foot.

Gruppenbild ohne Dame

AFTER AUGUST SANDER

1923, gathering Depression. In this interior
in Cologne, it's Laocoön all over again.
This time, Fate has left him his two boys
and taken his wife.—Though it is difficult
to see how a woman could have fitted in, here:
a road winding in an empty landscape on the wall,
the threadbare carpet, and one hard Sunday chair.
. . . A male Trinity, the Father and his two Sons.
The maculate conceptions of his bald head.
Baby watchchains like Papa's, and knickerbockers
aspiring to the condition of his three-piece suit.
Their knotty skulls show a family likeness,
heads shaved for lice and summer—skinny boys
with their mother's big eyes and hurt mouth.

Family Holidays

The car got a sun-tan while my father worked
in its compound . . . Mixed with the cicadas,
you could hear the fecundity of his typing
under the green corrugated plastic roof.

My mother staggered about like a nude
in her sun-hat, high heels and bathing-costume.
She was Quartermaster and Communications.

My doughy sisters baked on the stony beach,
swelling out of their bikinis, turning over
every half-hour. Still, they were never done.

The little one fraternised with foreign children.

. . . Every day I swam further out of my depth,
but always, miserably, crawled back to safety.

The Magic of Mantovani

die Vergänglichkeit begegnete ihm als Musik.

—GÜNTER EICH, 'Handel'

The invited audience applauds on cue—
steady couples in their late twenties,
well-dressed and supplied with contraceptives.

A giant in the world of light music, they say;
so much happiness in those globe-trotting tunes . . .
The surf of percussion. Swaying in treetops,

violins hold the high notes. Careful brass
for the darker moments—the blood of Spain.
The accordion is a European capital . . .

A sentimental music, porous with associations,
it played in the dimness before the ads,
when I went to the cinema with my father.

He disappeared into his own thoughts, abstracted,
rubbing his fingers together under his nose . . .
Scattered in the red plush of the cinema,

a handful of people were waiting for the feature.
Regular constellations of stars twinkled
on the ceiling while daylight wasted outside.

Ice cream was no longer on sale in the foyer—
the end of kindness . . . I thought about mortality,
and cried for my father's inevitable death.

Boys' Own

I. M. TREVOR PARK

A parting slightly off-centre, like Oscar Wilde's,
his fat mouth, and the same bulky appearance.
Your hair was pomaded, an immaculate wet-look,
sculpted and old-fashioned in these blow-dry times.
The dull grain of wood on polished furniture.
—Everyone has an inspiring English teacher
somewhere behind them, and you were ours. We argued
about you: that your smell was not sweet after-shave,
but the presbyterian rigours of cold water—

on your porous face and soft, womanish hands . . . ?
The public-school teacher has to be versatile—
if not the genuine Renaissance article, then at least
a modern pentathlete—and so you appeared to us
in as many guises as an Action Man: for lessons,
with a gown over one of your heavy three-piece suits;
wearing khaki for Corps on Wednesday afternoons;
as a soccer referee in a diabolical black tracksuit;
in baggy but respectable corduroys on holidays . . .

Morning coffee was followed by pre-prandial sherry
after only the shortest of intervals. The empties,
screw-tops, stood in boxes outside your door.

You drank early, copiously, and every day—
though it hardly crossed our minds. Given the chance,
we would have done too . . . It was 'civilised',
and that was what you were about. Sweet and sour sherry,
lager on warm afternoons, the pathos of sparkling wine
for occasions. 'It's actually quite like champagne . . .'

Just as an extension-lead went from your gramophone
to its little brother, a 'stereophonic' loudspeaker—
Ferguson Major and Minor . . . With one hand in your pocket,
leaning back in your swivelling chair, you conducted
your own records, legs double-crossed like Joyce's.
—Among all those other self-perpetuating oddball
bachelors, how could we fail to understand you?
Your military discipline and vintage appearance,
the sublimation of your Anglicanism, your drinking . . .

We only waited for that moment at the end of a class,
when, exhausted by intellectual inquiry, you took off
your glasses and rubbed away your tiny blue eyes . . .
All of love and death can be found in books;
you would have agreed. At one of your 'gatherings',
someone found a pubic hair in your sheepskin rug . . .
Years later, there was a scandal, an ultimatum,
and you threw yourself under the wheels of a train—
the severe way Tolstoy chose for Anna Karenina.

Lord B. and Others

Yoghurt and garlic pills, Balkan products
that feed on the myth of immortality
in South Eastern Europe; based on
the continuing survival of generations
of gypsy violinists and fortune-tellers
born before the birth certificate . . .
A weather-beaten old gent on a poster
in a chemist's shop; glaring; below him,
his ambiguous life-enhancing statement:
'It's not how old you are that matters,
it's how old you feel.' Crossing the Alps,
the spectre of Shelley's sister-in-law
following him, pregnant with his child,
Byron stopped at an inn and surrendered
his passport; then entered name and address
on the printed form, giving his age as
'a hundred'. When he died, eight years later,
still only thirty-six, his heart and brain
were accordingly found to be quite used up—
'those of an old man', a devout particular
in his French romancier's biography.

By Forced Marches

Who knows what would happen if you stopped?
The autobiography draws out, lengthens
towards the end. Life stays in one place,
often Rome; and to compensate, you cut up
your time in many pieces. Rations are halved,
then quartered. The emergency is acute.
Now it is one lump of sugar per day.

l'an trentiesme de son eage

CÔTE D'AZUR, 1919

Ospedaletti. The little hospitals—
a makeshift sanatorium for one,
despite a wicked climate of cold and wind.
A few miles down the coast, the weather
is far milder—the French Riviera just then
coming into fashion: Monte Carlo, Nice,
Menton with its Mansfield memorial . . .
St Tropez was a fishing port until
Brigitte Bardot put it on the map,
years later, by going around topless.
K.M. has TB. With her is 'L.M.', alias
Ida Baker. K.M. criticizes her incessantly—
one disagreeable feature of her illness.
It's hardly the scandalous lesbian affair
you read about, but a sad, bitchy one . . .
Her spendthrift nature; no intellectual
or personal stimulus to be got from her;
the sheer banality of her appearance—
her tiny blind breasts, her baby mouth,
the underlip always wet and a crumb or two
or a chocolate stain at the corners . . .
God knows there are enough adversities besides.

—The gardener is a rogue: charging extra
for flowers he promised to supply free.
Like everything else, they are for Murry,
her husband. They have never really lived
together. She wants to lure him back to her,
but he is in England, advancing his career
as a man of letters . . . She wrote to him,
I love you more than ever now I am 31.

Shapes of Things

We are living in the long shadow of the Bomb—
a fat Greenpeace whale, simplified and schematic
like the sign 'lavatories for the handicapped',
its whirling genitals a small outboard swastika . . .

I saw the rare Ava Gardner, the last woman alive,
modelling her check workshirts in *On the Beach*.
As the wind drove the heavy clouds of fallout
towards them, there were no ugly scenes of anarchy—

only revivalist preachers and the Salvation Army band . . .
She admired the *esprit de corps* of her husband
as he went down in the last living submarine—
an obsolete nuclear cigar, doused in the bay.

Furth i. Wald

FOR JAN AND ANJA T.

There are seagulls inland, extensive flooding
and a grey sky. A tractor stalled in midfield
between two goals. Mammoth sawmills collecting trees
and pulping them for furniture and wallpaper . . .
These strips of towns, with their troubled histories,
they are lost in the woods like Hansel and Gretel.
Counters at peace conferences, they changed hands
so often, they became indistinguishable, worthless.
Polyglot and juggled like Belgium, each of them keeps
a spare name in the other language to fall back on.
Only their wanton, spawning frontier tells them apart,
an arrogant line of wire in an electric clearing.
(A modern derivative of the civic myth of Thebes:
the oxhide cut into ribbons by cunning estate agents,
and laid end to end; so many towns called Cuernavaca . . .)
—At other frontiers, it may be a long tunnel instead,
too long for you to hold your breath. At halfway,
the texture of the concrete changes, and the lights,
but you can't say where it is brighter or safer . . .
Nations are irregular parcels, tight with fear.
But their contents have settled during transport.
Grenzflucht. Perimeters that are now deserted and

timid, the dream-wrappings clash with each other.
On one side, the lonely heartless villas of the guards.
Dustbins stored like sandbags outside barrackrooms.
The play of searchlights . . . On the other, *Der Neue
Tag* dawns only twice a week nowadays. With its
progressive-sounding name and millenarian ideals, still
holding the fort for a dwindling readership . . .

On Fanø

Acid rain from the Ruhr strips one pine in three . . .
To supplement their living, the neutral Danes
let out their houses during the summer months—
exposure, convexity, clouds and the shadows of clouds.
Wild grass grows on the manure of their thatch.

There are concrete bunkers among the sand dunes—
bomb shelters, or part of Heligoland and the V2s . . . ?
German hippies have taken them over, painted them
with their acid peace dreams; a cave art of
giant people, jungles, a plague of dragonflies.

Fates of the Expressionists

The Kaiser was the first cousin of George V,
descended, as he was, from *German* George,
and unhappy Albert, the hard-working Saxon Elector.
—The relaxed, navy-cut beard of the one,
hysterical, bristling moustaches of the other . . .
The Expressionists were Rupert Brooke's generation.
Their hold on life was weaker than a baby's.
Their deaths, at whatever age, were infant mortality—
a bad joke in this century. Suddenly become sleepy,
they dropped like flies, whimsical, sizzling,
ecstatic, from a hot light-bulb. Even before the War,
Georg Heym and a friend died in a skating accident.
From 1914, they died in battle and of disease—
or suicide like Trakl. *Drugs Alcohol Little Sister.*
One was a student at Oxford and died, weeks later,
on the other side . . . Later, they ran from the Nazis.
Benjamin was turned back at the Spanish border—
his history of the streets of Paris unfinished—
deflected into an autistic suicide. In 1938,
Ödön von Horváth, author of naturalistic comedies,
was struck by a falling tree. In Paris.

                         At the time
my anthology was compiled, there were still a few left:
unexplained survivors,

                     psychoanalysts in the New World.

Nights in the Iron Hotel

Our beds are at a hospital distance.
I push them together. Straw matting
on the walls produces a Palm Beach effect:

long drinks made with rum in tropical bars.
The position of mirror and wardrobe
recalls a room I once lived in happily.

Our feelings are shorter and faster now.
You confess a new infidelity. This time,
a trombone player. His tender mercies . . .

All night, we talk about separating.
The radio wakes us with its muzak.
In a sinister way, you call it lulling.

We are fascinated by our own anaesthesia,
our inability to function. Sex is a luxury,
an export of healthy physical economies.

The TV stays switched on all the time.
Dizzying socialist realism for the drunks.
A gymnast swings like a hooked fish.

(PRAGUE)

Body Heat

This evening belongs to a warmer day—
separated clouds, birds, bits of green . . .
We wake late, naked, stuck to each other:
the greenhouse effect of windows and bedclothes.

Fifty years late, you finish *Love on the Dole*.
—Who knows, perhaps it can really be done?
The Boots hair-setting gel no longer works;
your pecker is down. The underdog's leather jacket

is here to stay, the stubborn lower lip
of the disconsolate punk . . . The poor hedgehogs,
they must help each other to pull off the leaves
that covered them while they were hibernating.

FROM

ACRIMONY

(1986)

Ancient Evenings

FOR A.

My friends hunted in packs, had themselves photographed
under hoardings that said 'Tender Vegetables'
or 'Big Chunks', but I had you—my Antonia!
Not for long, nor for a long time now . . .

Later, your jeans faded more completely,
and the hole in them wore to a furred square,
as it had to, but I remember my hands
skating over them, there where the cloth was thickest.

You were so quiet, it seemed like an invitation
to be disturbed, like Archimedes and the soldier,
like me, like the water displaced from my kettle
when I heated tins of viscous celery soup in it

until the glue dissolved and the labels crumbled
and the turbid, overheated water turned into more soup . . .
I was overheated, too. I could not trust my judgement.
The coffee I made in the dark was eight times too strong.

My humour was gravity, so I sat us both in an armchair
and toppled over backwards. I must have hoped
the experience of danger would cement our relationship.
Nothing was broken, and we made surprisingly little noise.

On the Margins

FOR XANDRA BINGLEY

Hospitality and unease, weekend guests
in this Chekhovian rectory painted a frivolous
blush pink. It is comfortable and fallen,
as though run by children, but with an adult's
guiding hand for basics, food, warmth, light . . .
At other times, what conversations, what demeanours!
I stare at myself in the grey, oxidised mirror
over the fireplace, godless, inept, countrified.
The distance disappears between rooms and voices.
Stuffy and centripetal, I tag after my hosts,
talking, offering 'help', sitting on tables
or leaning ungraciously in the doorway.

We drove twenty miles to buy roses, to a stately home
behind a moat and a pair of netted Alsatians.
The shaggy, youthful master of the house
was already onto his second family. His little boy
must have guessed. He had the exemplary energy
of the late child, working on his parents' stamina,
boisterous and surexcited, running to fetch us
prayer books, one at a time, they were so heavy.

Back here, I feel again spiritless, unhappy, the wrong age.
Not to be condescended to, still less fit for equality.
I quarrel with you over your word 'accomplished',
and then slink off upstairs to make it up . . .
We hear the hoarse, see-saw cries of the donkeys
grazing in the churchyard, mother and daughter,
and the first mosquitoes bouncing up and down,
practising their verticals like a video game. Next door,
his green clothes hung on pegs, Eric, the rustic burr,
is taking a bath, whistling and crooning happily
in his timeless, folkloric voice. I pat your nakedness.
In evil whispers, I manage to convince you.

Changes

Birds singing in the rain, in the dawn chorus,
on power lines. Birds knocking on the lawn,
and poor mistaken worms answering them . . .

They take no thought for the morrow, not like you
in your new job.—It paid for my flowers, now
already stricken in years. The stiff cornflowers

bleach, their blue rinse grows out. The marigolds
develop a stoop and go bald, orange clowns,
straw polls, their petals coming out in fistfuls . . .

Hard to take you in your new professional pride—
a salary, place of work, colleagues, corporate spirit—
your new *femme d'affaires* haircut, hard as nails.

Say I must be repressive, afraid of castration,
loving the quest better than its fulfilment.
—What became of you, bright sparrow, featherhead?

Aerial Perspective

Where the picturesque collides with the strategically
important, in some dog-eared, dog-rose corner
of Cornwall or Suffolk, there's a clutch of airbases,
and a weekend cottage called Boeing's Rest . . .

I can only hear the big AWACS aircraft
homing back in the fog across the North Sea—
tailplanes like leg-nutcrackers, and ridden by
their great, rotating, white-striped black toadstools—

but no doubt they can see us blips, as they can see
the blind gophers chewing up the putting-surface,
and the discarded copy of *Pull* or *Weapon* lying in a hole
in the road: men at work, a reassuring sight.

A Floating City

Un seul être vous manque, et tout est dépeuplé. —LAMARTINE

After the card-players, the cuba libre drinkers
and the readers of two-day-old newspapers,
there are the night strollers, pastel shades down the bobble-lit
Atlantic esplanade, by the small roar of the waves.

We saw the passenger liner put in for the afternoon,
then put out again: a floating city, heading South,
then pulling a slow turn, end on to the shore,
and backing North-West for the Azores or the shipping-lanes—

a wide and wasteful curve, elegiac and deceptive,
like that of your plane (and its decoy), that I followed
standing in the jetstream as they lifted away,
penny-pinching Britannias on their chartered tails . . .

The place was demolished in an earthquake and rebuilt
on a new site: built down, having learned its lesson,
wide and flat, built for cars.—With you gone out of it,
it seems destroyed again, and rebuilt to less purpose.

I stand on Avenue Mohammed V like a crowd hoping for
     a motorcade.
When the King comes to stay, he's like an earthquake,
living with the one thing his paranoia can live with,
the migrant population he calls an entourage.

A Brief Occupation

Six floors up, I found myself like a suicide—
one night, the last thing in a bare room . . .
I was afraid I might frighten my neighbours,
two old ladies dying of terror, thinking
every man was the gasman, every gasman a killer . . .

I was not myself. I was just anyone. The next day,
the place was going to be sold. Every so often,
high-spirited car horns bypassed the dead-end street.
The outside wall was a slowly declining roof,
an electricity meter clung to life by a few threads . . .

There was an inhuman shortage of cloth in that room:
a crocheted rug with a few eloquent hairs on it,
a stone for a pillow, my coat hanging demurely in the window.
The hairs belonged to a girl, now back in Greece,
an island, a museum of mankind.

Entr'acte

The enemies of democracy were back supporting it.
Soldiers went in fear of their MPs, looked slippy
on the parade ground, tumbling from their personnel carriers,
parleyed in groups of two and three with girls at the gate.

I sat and picnicked on my balcony, no picnic,
eyeing the tarmac through the rusty gridiron underfoot,
flicking ash and wincing at my pips going lickety-split,
hitting the deck fifty feet down, among the sentries.

Inside, the wall met neither floor nor ceiling.
Two stripes of light reached into my room from next door,
where I heard an American girl—mezzo, ardent—
crying, 'Don't come, sweet Jesus, not yet.'

Nighthawks

FOR JAMES LASDUN

Time isn't money, at our age, it's water.
You couldn't say we cupped our hands very tightly . . .
We missed the second-last train, and find ourselves
at the station with half an hour to kill.

The derelicts queue twice round the tearoom.
Outside, the controlled prostitutes move smoothly
through the shoals of men laughing off their fear.
The street-lamps are a dull coral, snakes' heads.

Earlier, I watched a couple over your shoulder.
She was thin, bone-chested, dressed in black lace,
her best feature vines of hair. Blatant, ravenous,
post-coital, they greased their fingers as they ate.

I met a dim acquaintance, a man with the manner
of a laughing-gas victim, rich, frightened and jovial.
Why doesn't everyone wear pink, he squeaked.
Only a couple of blocks are safe in his world.

Now we've arrived at this hamburger heaven,
a bright hole walled with mirrors where our faces show
pale and evacuated in the neon. We spoon our sundaes
from a metal dish. The chopped nuts are poison.

We've been six straight hours together, my friend,
sitting in a shroud of earnestness and misgiving.
Swarthy, big-lipped, suffering, tubercular,
your hollow darkness survives even in this place . . .

The branch-line is under the axe, but it still runs,
rattling and screeching, between the hospital
lit like a toy, and the castellated factory—
a folie de grandeur of late capitalism.

From Kensal Rise to Heaven

Old Labour slogans, *Venceremos*, dates for demonstrations
like passed deadlines—they must be disappointed
to find they still exist. Halfway down the street,
a sign struggles to its feet and says Brent.

*

The surfaces are friable, broken and dirty, a skin unsuitable
for chemical treatment. Building, repair and demolition
go on simultaneously, indistinguishably. Change and decay.
—When change is arrested, what do you get?

*

The Sun, our Chinese takeaway, is being repainted.
I see an orange topcoat calls for a pink undercoat.
A Chinese calendar girl, naked, chaste and varnished,
simpers behind potplants like a jungle dawn.

*

Joy, local, it says in the phone-booth, with a number
next to it. Or *Petra*. Or *Out of Order*, and an arrow.
This last gives you pause, ten minutes, several weeks . . .
Delay deters the opportunist as much as doubt.

*

In an elementary deception, the name of the street
is taken from a country town, and when I get up
I find my education is back to haunt me: Dickens House,
Blake Court, Austen House, thirteen-storey giants.

*

Some Sunday mornings, blood trails down the street
from the night before. Stabbing, punch-up or nosebleed,
it's impossible to guess, but the drops fell thickly and easily
on the paving-stones, too many for the rules of hopscotch.

*

The roadway itself is reddish, the faded spongy brick
of the terrace is overpowered by the paintwork's
sweet dessert colours. They spoil it, but you understand
they are there as the sugar in tomato soup is there.

*

Clouds come over from the West, as always in England
the feeling that the sea is just beyond the next horizon:
a thick, Byzantine crucifix on a steep schoolhouse roof,
the slippery, ecclesiastical gleam of wet slate.

*

Dogs vet the garbage before the refuse collectors.
Brazen starlings and pigeons, 'flying rats', go over
what is left. Rough-necked, microcephalous, they have
too much white on their bodies, like calcium defectives.

*

The pigeons mate in full view: some preliminary billing,
then the male flutters his wings as though to break a fall . . .
They inhabit a ruined chiropodist's, coming and going freely
through broken windows into their cosy excremental hollow.

*

The old man in the vest in the old people's home
would willingly watch us all day. In their windows,
a kind of alcove, they keep wine bottles and candlesticks,
Torvill and Dean, a special occasion on ice.

*

The motor-mews has flat roofs of sandpaper or tarpaper.
One is terraced, like three descending trays of gravel.
Their skylights are angled towards the red East,
some are truncated pyramids, others whole glazed shacks.

Open House

Rawlplugs and polyfilla ... the cheerful,
tamping thump of reggae through the floorboards,

the drawling vowel 'r' of Irish or Jamaican English
carrying easily through the heated, excitable air—

as though I lived in a museum without walls.

This Sporting Death

The days are so dark they hardly count—
but they must have some marginal warmth after all,
for the drizzle of my night-breath turns to fog.

The window is opaque, a white mirror affirming
life goes on inside this damp lung of a room . . .
I have no perspective on the dotty winter clouds,

the pubic scrub of this street I am growing to hate,
with its false burglar alarms and sleeping policemen.
My exhalations blot out the familiar view.

I can tell without looking when your car draws up,
I know its tune as it reaches the end of its tether
and stops under the lamp-post, melodramatic and old-red,

the unwilling gift of your sainted grandmother
who disliked you and died suddenly on Friday.
'Grand-merde' you called her when you left sometimes

to go with her to visit your uncle in hospital,
lying there with irreversible brain damage
almost as long as I've lived here, after

falling downstairs drunk. You chat to him,
and imagine or fail to imagine that he responds
when you play him the recording of his greatest moment

when the horse he trained won the Derby.
I stay here and listen to sport on the radio,
a way of processing time to trial and outcome.

Someone brought me some cigarettes from America
called *Home Run*, and they frighten me half to death
in their innocuous vernal packaging, green and yellow.

Kif

The filter crumples—a cruel exhilaration
as the day's first cigarette draws to a close.
The optician's colours turn to a dizzy whiteness
in my solar plexus . . . With longing I speculate
on Heimito von Doderer's excursus on tobacco—
the pharmaceutical precision of the true scholar.

Disturbances

I go over to my window in South Cambridge,
where the Official Raving Loony Monster candidate
stands to poll half a per cent—the moral majority . . .

Below me, the idyllic lilac tree has scorched
to beehive, to beeswax, to *Bienenstich*, a spongy cack.
Voorman parks his purple car in its shade.

I picture him underneath it, his helter-skelter
fat-man jeans halfway down, showing his anal cleft.
Though what would he be doing, face down like that?!

He's even more remote than I am, curtains drawn,
stopping the plug-hole with his hair-loss,
never a letter for him, a visit or a phone call.

How is it, then, that in the featurelessness
of his Sundays he throws fits, shouting and swearing,
punching the walls, putting us in fear of our lives?

I'm so fearful and indecisive, all my life
has been in education, higher and higher education . . .
What future for the fly with his eye on the flypaper?

The house is breaking up, and still I'm hanging on here:
scaffolding and a skip at the door, smells of dust
and sawdust, the trepanation of the floorboards.

Between Bed and Wastepaper Basket

There hasn't been much to cheer about in three years
in this boxroom shaped like a loaf of bread,
the flimsy partitions of the servants' quarters,
high up in the draughty cranium of the house.

All things tend towards the yellow of unlove,
the tawny, moulting carpet where I am commemorated
by tea- and coffee-stains, by the round holes of furniture—
too much of it, and too long in the same place.

Here, we have been prepared for whatever comes next.
The dishonest, middle-aged anorexic has been moved on.
The radio buff is now responsible for contact
in the cardboard huts of the British Antarctic Survey.

(His great antenna was demolished here one stormy night.)
The tiny American professor is looking for tenure.
On occasional passionate weekends, the vinegary
smell of cruel spermicide carried all before it.

Familiarity breeds mostly the fear of its loss.
In winter, the ice-flowers on the inside of the window
and the singing of the loose tap; in summer,
the thunderflies that came in and died on my books

like bits of misplaced newsprint . . . I seize the day
when you visited me here—the child's world in person:
gold shoes, grass skirt, sky blouse and tinted, cirrus hair.
We went outside. Everything in the garden was rosy.

Prefabs ran down the back of the Applied Psychology Unit.
Pigeons dilated. The flies were drowsy from eating
the water-lilies on the pond. A snake had taken care of
the frogs. Fuchsias pointed their toes like ballerinas.

My hand tried to cup your breast. You were jail-bait,
proposing a miraculous career as county wife
and parole officer. We failed to betray
whatever trust was placed in us.

Campaign Fever

We woke drugged and naked. Did our flowers
rob us and beat us over the head while we were asleep?
They were competing for the same air as us—
the thick, vegetable breath of under the eaves.

It seems like several days ago that I went
to see you to your train. A cuckoo called
and our vision drizzled, though the air was dry.
In a place I'd never noticed before, a low siren

was sounding alternate notes. I remembered
it had been going all night. Was it in distress?
I slept four times, and ate with the base,
groundless haste of someone eating alone.

Afterwards I smoked a cigarette and lay on my back
panting, as heavy and immobile as my own saliva.
The newspapers preyed on my mind. On the radio,
the National Front had five minutes to put their case.

The fiction of an all-white Albion, deludedness
and control, like my landlady's white-haired old bitch,
who confuses home with the world, pees just inside the door
and shits trivially in a bend in the corridor.

Mr Thatcher made his pile by clearing railway lines
with sheep-dip (the millionaire's statutory one idea).
When he sold his shares, they grew neglected,
plants break out and reclaim the very pavements . . .

I think of you trundling across Middle England,
Peterborough, Leicester, Birmingham New Street—
the onetime marginals—up to your eyes in a vigorous,
delinquent haze of buttercups, milfoil and maple scrub.

Day of Reckoning

When we drove across America, going West,
I tanned through the sandwich glass windscreen.
Though I was eight, and my legs weren't yet long
in their long pants, I could still sit in front—

your co-driver who couldn't spell you . . .
My jagged elbow stuck out the right-hand window,
I kept a tough diary, owned a blunt knife,
and my mother sat in the back with the girls.

I can't remember if we talked, or if, even then,
you played the radio, but when I got tired
I huddled in my legroom in the Chevy Bel Air,
and watched the coloured stars under the dashboard . . .

I learned fractions from you in a single day,
multiplying and dividing. In Kingston, Ontario,
I had a cruel haircut. For you, it was a dry time—
in two years one short play about bankruptcy:

Let Them Down, Gently. There followed the great crash.

The Machine That Cried

Il n'y a pas de détail. —PAUL VALÉRY

When I learned that my parents were returning
to Germany, and that I was to be jettisoned,
I gave a sudden lurch into infancy and Englishness.
Carpets again loomed large in my world: I sought out
their fabric and warmth, where there was nowhere to fall . . .

I took up jigsaw puzzles, read mystical cricket thrillers
passing all understanding, even collected toy soldiers
and killed them with matchsticks fired from the World War One
field-guns I bought from Peter Oborn down the road
—he must have had something German, with that name—

who lived alone with his mother, like a man . . .
My classmates were equipped with sexual insults
for the foaming lace of the English women playing Wimbledon,
but I watched them blandly on our rented set
behind drawn curtains, without ever getting the point.

My building-projects were as ambitious as the Tower of Babel.
Something automotive of my construction limped across the floor
to no purpose, only lugging its heavy battery.
Was there perhaps some future for Christiaan Barnard,
or the electric car, a milk-float groaning like a sacred heart?

I imagined Moog as von Moog, a mad German scientist.
His synthesiser was supposed to be the last word in versatility,
but when I first heard it on Chicory Tip's
Son of My Father, it was just a unisono metallic drone,
five notes, as inhibited and pleonastic as the title.

My father bought a gramophone, a black box,
and played late Beethoven on it, which my mother was always
to associate with her miscarriage of that year.
I was forever carrying it up to my room,
and quietly playing through my infant collection of singles,

Led Zeppelin, The Tremoloes, My Sweet Lord . . .
The drums cut like a scalpel across the other instruments.
Sometimes the turntable rotated slowly, then everything
went flat, and I thought how with a little more care
it could have been all right. There again, so many things

were undependable . . . My first-ever British accent wavered
between Pakistani and Welsh. I called Bruce's record shop
just for someone to talk to. He said, 'Certainly, Madam.'
Weeks later, it was 'Yes sir, you can bring your children.'
It seemed I had engineered my own birth in the new country.

My Father's House Has Many Mansions

Who could have said we belonged together,
my father and my self, out walking, our hands held
behind our backs in the way Goethe recommended?

Our heavy glances tipped us forward—the future,
a wedge of pavement with our shoes in it . . .
In your case, beige, stacked, echoing clogs;

and mine, the internationally scruffy tennis shoes—
seen but not heard—of the protest movement.
My mother shook her head at us from the window.

I was taller and faster but more considerate:
tense, overgrown, there on sufferance, I slowed down
and stooped for you. I wanted to share your life.

Live with you in your half-house in Ljubljana,
your second address: talk and read books;
meet your girlfriends, short-haired, dark, oral;

go shopping with cheap red money in the supermarket;
share the ants in the kitchen, the unfurnished rooms,
the fallible winter plumbing. Family was abasement

and obligation ... The three steps to your door
were three steps to heaven. But there were only visits.
At a party for your students—my initiation!—

I ceremoniously downed a leather glass of *slivovica*.
But then nothing. I wanted your mixture of resentment
and pride in me expanded to the offer of equality.

Is the destination of paternity only advice ... ?
In their ecstasy of growth, the bushes along the drive
scratch your bodywork, dislocate your wing-mirror.

Every year, the heraldic plum-tree in your garden
surprises you with its small, rotten fruit.

Bärli

Your salami breath tyrannised the bedroom
where you slept on the left, my mother, tidily,
on the right. I could cut the atmosphere with a knife:

the enthusiasm for spice, rawness, vigour,
in the choppy air. It was like your signature,
a rapid scrawl from the side of your pen—

individual, overwhelming, impossible—
a black Greek energy that cramped itself into
affectionate diminutives, *Dein Vati*, or *Papi*.

At forty, you had your tonsils out, child's play
with Little Bear nuns, Ursulines for nurses.
Hours after the operation, you called home . . .

humbled and impatient, you could only croak.
I shivered at your weakness—the faint breeze
that blew through you and formed words.

Lighting Out

Business, independence, a man alone, travelling—
I was on your territory. Though what I represented
was not myself, but a lawnmower manufacturer,
whipping round the green belts in Northern Germany.

Hardly your line, then—that would have been
a tour of radio stations, or public readings—
but once I swanned off to mercantile Lübeck, and saw
Thomas Mann's ugly Nobel plaque, and the twin towers

on fifty-mark banknotes. And I coincided
with the publication of your firstborn, The Denunciation.
I proudly bought a copy on my expenses, giving you
your first royalties on twenty-odd years of my life . . .

But being a salesman was dispiriting work. I ran myself
like an organisation, held out the prospect of bonuses,
wondered which of the tiny, sad, colourful bottles
in my freezing minibar I would crack next.

Vortex

Where was our high-water mark? Was it the glorious
oriental scimitar in the Metropolitan Museum
in New York? Nothing for a pussyfooting shake-hands grip:
your hand had to be a fist already to hold it . . .
I wondered why the jewels were all clustered
on scabbard and hilt and basketed hand-guard,
why there were none on the sword itself.
I could only guess that the blade leapt out
to protect them, like a strong father his family.

—Or next door, where, as the guide explained,
there was a deity in the ceiling, who would shower
genius or intellect or eyewash on those beneath?
And straightaway, to my fierce embarrassment,
you pushed me under it, an un-European moment—
though I tried also to relish the shiver of limelight.

—Or was it more even, less clinching, the many years
I used the basin after you had shaved in it?
It was my duty to shave the basin, rinsing
the circle of hairs from its concave enamel face
till it was as smooth as yours . . . I was almost there,
on the periphery of manhood, but I didn't have your gear:

the stiff brush of real badger (or was it beaver?);
the reserved cake of shaving soap; the safety razor
that opened like Aladdin's cave when I twirled the handle.
. . . That movement became an escape mechanism:
I was an orphan, a street Arab, waiting for you
in international lounges, at the foot of skyscrapers;
entertaining myself with the sprinkler nozzles
secreted in the ceiling, whirling dervishes
sniffing out smoke, in a state of permanent readiness;
or with the sprung, centrifugal, stainless ashtrays
that have since emancipated me, like the razors
—cheapskate, disposable, no moving parts—
I now use myself . . . The water drains away, laughing.
I light up, a new man.

Withdrawn from Circulation

My window gave on to a street-corner where the air currents
(*Berliner Luft!*) were of such bewildering complexity
that the snow, discouraged, fell back up the sky . . .

It stayed shut, and I sweated in the central heat
as I sweated in my pyjamas at night, snug as a worm
in my slithery tapering orange-and-green sleeping bag.

For a whole month, the one soiled bedsheet
was supposed to knit together, to join in matrimony
the shiny blue tripartite mattress, borrowed or looted

from a ruined office, but good as new.
Small wonder I hugged it in sleep! On the floor
lay the door that was to have made me a table.

It was said there was nothing between here and Siberia—
except Poland—but indoors was the tropics.
I was eighteen, and frittering away.

I picked up just enough politics to frighten my mother,
and the slick, witless phrases I used about girls
were a mixture of my father's and those I remembered

from *Mädchen* or *Bravo* . . . Nothing quite touched me.
I put on weight, smoked Players and read Dickens
for anchorage and solidity. Come the autumn,

I was going to Cambridge. A few doors down
was the cellar where the RAF kept the Berlin Senator
they had kidnapped and were holding to ransom.

From time to time, his picture appeared
in the newspapers, authenticated by other newspapers
in the picture with him. He was news that stayed news.

(KREUZBERG)

Giro Account

Out of the pornographic cinema at the station,
with the fast clock and the continuous programme,
then past the French sweet-stall, the naturist magazines

and the cretin at the lottery ticket-office
—*das schnelle Glück*: a quick buck or fuck—
and into the night train to Berlin . . .

It was sealed and non-stop, but East German border guards
woke us up so they could give us our transit visas,
and then it was early on Sunday, and I walked

out of *Berlin-Zoo* in my father's lion coat,
his suitcase in one hand and his bag in the other.
I was nineteen and a remittance man,

embarked on a delirium of self-sufficiency,
surprised that it was possible to live like a bird:
to stay in a hotel, to eat in restaurants,

and draw my father's money from a giro account.
At the end of my feeding-tube, I didn't realise
that to stay anywhere on the earth's surface is to bleed:

money, attention, effort . . . It was no problem.
I avoided my companions—the cold young man
with the Inca cap, the weak heart and the blue face,

his obese, scatologically-brained sister—and stared
incessantly at a Peruvian woman in a nightclub.
There was a girl who one day told me she'd become engaged.

The motherly hotel manageress gave me the rolls
left over from my breakfast for the rest of the day.
Once, she gave me my father on the telephone.

I asked him about his conference, but he wanted
something else: to have me at the end of a telephone
line, an alibi, proof of my harmlessness—

he had become jealous of a spivvy young Englishman . . .
There was no crime, no conference, maybe no Englishman:
only my father, his son and his new novel plot.

Catechism

My father peers into the lit sitting-room
and says, 'Are you here?' . . . Yes, I am,
in one of his cloudy white leather armchairs,
with one foot not too disrespectfully on the table,
reading Horváth's *Godless Youth*. Without another word,
he goes out again, baffling and incommunicable,
the invisible man, dampening any speculation.

My Father at Fifty

Your mysterious economy blows the buttons
off your shirts, and permits overdrafts
at several foreign banks.—It must cost the earth.

Once I thought of you virtually as a savage,
atavistic, well-aligned, without frailties.
A man of strong appetites, governed by instinct.

You never cleaned your teeth, but they were perfect anyway
from a diet of undercooked meat; you gnawed the bones;
anything sweet you considered frivolous.

Your marvellous, single-minded regime, kept up
for years, of getting up at four or five,
and writing a few pages 'on an empty stomach',

before exposing yourself to words—whether
on the radio, in books or newspapers,
or just your own from the day before . . .

Things are different now. Your male discriminations
—meat and work—have lost their edge.
Your teeth are filled, an omnivorous sign.

Wherever you are, there is a barrage of noise:
your difficult breathing, or the blaring radio—
as thoughtless and necessary as breathing.

You have gone to seed like Third World dictators,
fat heads of state suffering horribly
from Western diseases whose name is Legion . . .

Your concentration is gone: every twenty minutes,
you go to the kitchen, or you call your wife
over some trifle. Bad-tempered and irritable,

you sedate yourself to save the energy
of an outburst. Your kidneys hurt, there is even
a red band of eczema starring your chest.

Your beard—the friend of the writer who doesn't smoke—
is shot with white . . . A Christmas card arrives
to ask why you don't have any grandchildren.

Author, Author

verba volant, scripta manent

Can this be all that remains—two or three weeks a year,
sitting at the opposite end of the dinner table from my father?

To listen to his breathing, more snorting than breathing,
puffing out air through his nose during mouthfuls,

chewing loudly with open mouth, without enjoyment,
uninhibited, inhibiting, his only talk, talk of food?

And to watch myself watching him, fastidious and disloyal,
feeling my muscles through my shirt—an open knife!

(My own part of the conversation, thin, witty, inaudible,
as though I'd spoken in asides for twenty-five years.)

To come back to him unannounced, at regular intervals,
one of two or three unselfsufficient, cryptic,

grown-up strangers he has fathered, and see again
his small silver mouth in his great grizzled face,

head and stomach grown to childlike proportions,
supported on his unchanging, teenager's legs . . .

To come upon by chance, while emptying the dustbin,
the ripped, glittery foil-wrapping of his heart-medicines,

multiplication times-tables of empty capsules,
dosages like police ammunition in a civil disturbance,

bought for cash over the counter and taken according to need—
like his sudden peremptory thirst for a quart of milk.

If sex is nostalgia for sex, and food nostalgia for food,
his can't be—what did a child of the War get to eat

that he would want to go on eating, and to share?
Standing in the road as the American trucks rolled by:

chewing-gum, cigarettes, canned herrings, a kick in the teeth.
(The way it is with dogs, and their first puppy nourishment:

potato peelings, or my maternal grandmother in East Germany,
and Chéri, her gay dog—pampered, shy, neurotic Chéri,

corrupted by affection, his anal glands spoiling with virginity—
she feeds him heart and rice, the only cooking she ever does.) . . .

After the age of fifty, a sudden flowering, half a dozen novels
in as many years—dialogue by other means: his main characters

maniacs, compulsive, virtuoso talkers, talkers for dear life,
talkers in soliloquies, notebooks, tape-recordings, last wills . . .

Hear him on the telephone, an overloud, forced bonhomie,
standing feet crossed, and one punishing the other for lying,

woken up once at midnight by a drunken critic
with his girlfriend hanging on the extension—

her sweet name not a name at all, but a blandishment—
finishing with promises, and his vestigial phrase of English

after ten years in England, 'Bye, bye.' Then going off to pee,
like the boys at my boarding school after fire-practice . . .

Till that time, I had a worshipful proximity with him,
companionable and idolatrous. If my nose wasn't hooked,

my hair not black and straight, my frame too long,
my fingers not squat and powerful, fitting the typewriter keys,

then it was my mother's fault, her dilution, her adulteration.
Home from England, I landed on a chequered pattern

of unwillingness and miserable advice. Not to take drugs,
not to treat my face with vinegar or lemon juice,

to make influential friends, and not to consort with others.
And, on interesting subjects, either a silence

or the interviewee's too-rapid turning to his own experience . . .
Perplexed, wounded, without confidence, I left him to himself,

first going round the block on a small-wheeled bicycle
in one of his leather jackets, like an elderly terror;

or, now, on walks with my mother in the shitty park
among the burghers: his duffel coat in the zoo of democracy.

A performance, like everything else . . . What's the point?
He wants only his car and his typewriter and his Magic Marker.

Every action he divides into small stages, every traffic light
on the way home, and each one he punctuates with a crucified 'So.'

I ask myself what sort of consummation is available?
Fight; talk literature and politics; get drunk together?

Kiss him goodnight, as though half my life had never happened?

Fine Adjustments

By now, it is almost my father's arm,
a man's arm, that lifts the cigarettes to my mouth
numbed by smoke and raw onions and chocolate milk.

I need calm, something to tranquillise me
after the sudden storm between us that left me shaking,
and with sticky palms . . . It only happens here,

where I blurt in German, dissatisfied and unproficient
amid the material exhilaration of abstract furniture,
a new car on the Autobahn, electric pylons walking

through the erasures in the Bayrischer Wald . . .
Once before, I left some lines of Joseph Roth
bleeding on your desk: 'I had no father—that is,

I never knew my father—but Zipper had one.
That made my friend seem quite privileged,
as though he had a parrot or a St Bernard.'

All at once, my nature as a child hits me.
I was a moving particle, like the skidding lights
in a film-still. Provoking and of no account,

I kept up a constant rearguard action, jibing,
commenting, sermonising. 'Why did God give me a voice,'
I asked, 'if you always keep the radio on?'

It was a fugitive childhood. Aged four, I was chased
round and round the table by my father, who fell
and broke his arm he was going to raise against me.

Old Firm

Father, the writer bird writes bird's nest soup—
a frail, disciplined structure, spun from its spittle
with bits of straw and dirt, then boiled with beaten eggs . . .
It kept us fed till we were big enough to leave the nest.

We walked, *à trois*, to the end of the road, for my bus
to Riem, and the plane to Gatwick, seemingly
chartered by the *Bierfest* . . . A sudden thunderstorm
turned us into a family group: mother under her umbrella,

you hiding in a phone box, kindly holding the door open,
and me, giving no protection, and pretending
not to seek any either, wet and deserting and plastered,
like the hair making itself scarce on your bad head . . .

That morning you played me an interview you gave in French,
a language you hadn't spoken in my lifetime,
literally not since my birth, when you'd been in Toulouse,
on French leave . . . Now, we joked about it—

you were easier to understand than the interviewer!
Who else understood? Your edgy, defeated laugh?
The modest, unhopeful evangelism of your final appeal
to the people of Montreal not to stop reading?

FROM

CORONA, CORONA

(1993)

Lament for Crassus

Who grows old in fifty pages of Plutarch:
mores, omens, campaigns, Marius at sixty,
fighting fit, working out on the Campus Martius?

It surely isn't me, pushing thirty, taking a life a night,
my head on a bookshelf, five shelves of books overhead,
the bed either a classic or remaindered?

—I read about Crassus, who owned most of Rome.
Crassus, the third man, the third triumvir,
the second term in any calculation.

Crassus, the pioneer of insuranburn,
with his architect slaves and firefighter slaves,
big in silver, big in real estate, big in personnel.

Crassus, who had his name linked with a Vestal Virgin,
but was only after her house in the suburbs.
Crassus of bread and suburbs and circuses,

made Consul for his circuses, Crassus
impresario, not Crassus *imperator*, Crassus
who tried to break the military-political nexus.

Crassus, the inventor of the demi-pension holiday,
holed up in a cave on the coast of Spain for a month,
getting his dinner put out for him, and a couple of slave girls.

Crassus, whose standards wouldn't rise on the final day,
who came out of his corner in careless black,
whose head was severed a day later than his son's.

The Late Richard Dadd, 1817–1886

The *Kentish Independent* of 1843
carried his pictures of his father, himself
and the scene of his crime. The first photo-journalist:
fairy-painter, father-slayer, poor, bad, mad Richard Dadd.

His extended Grand Tour took in the Holy Land
and ended in Bethlem Hospital, with its long panoptical
galleries, spider-plants, whippets and double-gaslights.
He had outlived himself at twenty-six . . .

There was one day he seemed to catch sunstroke.
He fancied the black, scorched beard of a sheik
would furnish him with some 'capital paintbrushes'.
Sailing up the Nile, on the *Hecate*,

they spent Christmas Day eating boiled eggs
and plum pudding, and playing cards for the captain's soul.
The temples at Luxor stood under a full moon, lightly boiled.
Sir Thomas got off to try and bag a crocodile.

The route up from Marseille went as the crow flies—
precipitately, a dash from ear to ear.
A fellow traveller let him play with his collar and tie,
until he pulled out 'an excellent English razor'.

There was his watercolour, 'Dead Camel',
and a series of drawings of his friends,
all with their throats cut,
Frith, Egg, Dadd, Phillip and O'Neill.

He saw himself as a catspaw, Osiris's right-hand man
on earth. His digs in Newman Street
contained three hundred eggs, and the earth
cracked when he walked on it.

Max Beckmann: 1915

Nurse, aesthetician and war-artist:
not unpatriotic, not unfeeling.
Calm—excitable. Noted yellow shell-holes,
the pink bones of a village steeple, a heated purple sky.
Bombardments. Tricks of the light. Graphic wounds.

An aviator overflew him in the rose night,
buzzed him, performed for him. Friend or foe? *Libellule!*
A room of his own in a villa. *Kriegsblick.*
Medics intellectually stimulating,
one, from Hamburg, familiar with his work.

A commission to decorate the baths
—an Oriental scene, how asinine!—
deserts, palmettos, oases, dead Anzacs, Dardanelles.
A second fresco, of the bath-house personnel.
One thousand male nudes per diem.

A prey to faces. Went for a squinting Cranach.
A man with half a head laughed at his sketches,
recognising his companions. ('He died today.')
'Several hours' tigerish combat, then gave up
the assault'; his description of a sitting.

Some *esprit de corps*. Marching songs
weirdly soothing, took him out of himself.
Ha, the amusing pretensions of a civilian
trying to commandeer a hotel room.
English prisoners, thirsty mudlarks, plucky, droll.

In the trenches the men had kissed their lives goodbye.
A ricochet, a sniper. In the midst of life.
Crosses plugging foxholes, stabbed into sandbags.
A man with a pistol, head down, intent, hunting rats.
Another, frying spuds on a buddy's grave.

The Flemish clocks told German time.
Sekt and Mosel to wash down the yellow *vin de pays*.
Dr Bonenfant, with his boozy babyface.
'We poor children.' A commission
to illustrate the army songbook. Invalided out.

Kurt Schwitters in Lakeland

Like nothing else in Tennessee. —WALLACE STEVENS

It was between greens (bowling, cricket),
but the graveyard had stayed immune, half-cut, and smelling
the yellow, abandoned smell of hay. A couple were casting
dead flowers into a wire trash-coop.

Kurt Schwitters's tombstone was hewn in straight lines,
klipp und klar, in the shape of a hat, brim—crown.
Unseasonable, but undeniably local,
someone had left a dozen daffodils.

The man had flown: a refugee,
then interned on the Isle of Man;
released, dead, exhumed, and returned to Germany,
to vote with his feet for the 1950s.

*

His *Merz* was nothing to do with pain or March:
it had been withdrawn from the *Kommerz- und Privatbank*.
Each day he caught the early bus to work,
climbed up to his barn through a jungle of rhododendrons,

and built on to his *Merzwall.*—It too was moved,
cased in a steel frame, and keelhauled down the hill.
The one thing still there that his hands had touched
was a stone on the sill

of the picture window that had been put in
in place of the wall. It had an air
of having been given a spin,
a duck, a drakkar, a curling-stone.

Marvin Gaye

He added the final 'e'
to counteract the imputation of homosexuality.
His father was plain Revd Gay, his son Marvin III.

He slept with his first hooker
in the army, coming off saltpetre.
He thought there was another word for 'virgin' that wasn't 'eunuch'.

Including duets, he had fifty-five chart entries.
His life followed the rhythm of albums and tours.
He had a 'couple of periods of longevity with a woman'.

He preached sex to the cream suits,
the halter tops and the drug-induced personality disorders.
When his hair receded, he grew a woolly hat and beard.

Success was the mother of eccentricity and withdrawal.
In Ostend he felt the eyes of the Belgians on him,
in Topanga someone cut the throats of his two Great Danes.

At forty-four, back in his parents' house,
any one of a number of Marvins might come downstairs.
A dog collar shot a purple dressing-gown, twice.

Sally

Bist du gesund? Nein, Herz, Schlaf, Verdauung. —FRANZ KAFKA

A blue button-through day, a pink, a black,
the little black dress, the bricks circulating
painfully through the central heating system,
sorrow, lust and peristalsis at three.

Freebird

One forms not the faintest inward attachment,
especially here in America.   —D. H. LAWRENCE

Six girls round the pool in Stranglers' weather,
tanning; then three; then one (my favourite!),
every so often misting herself
or taking a drink of ice water from a plastic beaker.

Only the pool shark ever swam,
humming, vacuuming debris, cleverly avoiding its tail.
The white undersides of the mockingbirds
flashed green when they flew over.

The setting was a blue by pink downtown development,
Southern hurricane architecture in matchwood:
live-oaks and love-seats, handymen and squirrels,
an electric grille and a siege mentality.

The soil was cedar chips, sprinkler heads and ants.
A few transplanted azaleas with difficulty flowered.
On watering days,
the air stank of artesian sulphur.

I was cuntstruck and fat. My tight chinos
came from a Second Avenue surplus store
that had an RPG dangling from the ceiling.
Grenada had been; the campus killings came later.

I lived in three bare rooms and a walk-in refrigerator.
The telephone kept ringing for Furniture World.
I looked at the dirty waves
breaking on the blue carpet and said not exactly.

A con-artist called Washington showed me Greek letters
carved in his huge upper arm, and the pest control man,
his cry of a soul in pain, switched
the clicking roach boxes under the sink.

The frat boy overhead gave it to his sorority girl
    steamhammer-style.
Someone turned up the Lynyrd Skynyrd,
the number with the seven-minute instrumental coda.
Her little screams petered out, *inachevée*.

Up in the Air

TO HUGO WILLIAMS

The sky was breaking, and I felt little less numb
than the alcoholic devotedly spooning
pâté from a tub; than the divorcee's station wagon
with its dog-haired sheepskin dogseat;
or the birds barking in the trees to greet the day . . .

There was a grey heron standing on a green bank.
'Soul survivors' spilled out of the *Titanic*
in their once-fluorescent sailing whites.
You only live once. The record sang 'My Girl',
but that was a lie. She only shucked my cigarette packet,

as she danced before my eyes like the alphabet,
mostly like the letter A . . . I was Ajax,
I had stolen another man's captive, slaughtered sheep
like a maniac, counted my friends till
I fell asleep, now I would have to swim for it

in the greasy, yellow, woollen waves . . .
The bass drum went like a heart, there was a pillow
curled in the bottom of it for anchorage.
Our finger-joints shook in the free air,
sheep's knuckle-bones dicing for the seamless garment.

Three hours flat out on the hotel candlewick,
blunting my creases, then off to the airport
with its complement of tiny, specialised, ministering
vehicles. I sat over the wing, riveted, wary,
remembering ring fingers and flying kites.

Wheels

Even the piss-artist, rocking back and forth
on the balls of his feet like a musical policeman,
is making an irreversible commitment . . . He shivers.

(The faith, application and know-how it takes
to do anything, even under controlled circumstances!)
I find in myself this absurd purposefulness;

walking through my house, I lean forward,
I lick my finger to open a door, to turn over a page,
or the page of a calendar, or an advent calendar.

It takes all day to read twenty pages,
and the day goes down in a blaze of television.
One blue day is much like another . . . The plane lands

with a mew of rubber and a few 'less-than' signs.
The ball, remembering who hit it, keeps going.
The choreographed car-chase is ruinously exciting,

but the wheels turn very slowly backwards,
to convince the viewer that, far from wasting time,
he's recreating himself. A Christmas Special!

From the great outdoors, there's the derision
of real cars, the honeyed drone of approachable taxis,
some man's immortal Jag, numbered DEBIT ...

How it must cut past the huddle of water-blue Inyacars,
lining the elbow of the road: smashed imperatives,
wheelchair hulls, rhombuses, stalled quartz.

Schönlaterngasse

Better never than late like the modern concrete
firetrap firegaps spacing the Austrian baroque, risi e pisi;
like the morgenstern lamp's flex leaking plastic links of gold,
leaving the cut-glass nightlight good enough to drink;
like the same tulip reproduction twice in our hapless room,
where the twelve lines of a spider-plant die without offshoot:
your period, which we both half-hoped wouldn't come.

Dean Point

It was some kind of quarry, a great excavation—
caterpillar treads, surface water, lumps of clay,
the mess of possibilities . . . It bore the forbidden,
almost criminal aspect of industrial premises.

Ramps led down from one level circle to another,
three or four turns of a gigantic blunt screw.
Corrugated iron towers passed among themselves
on conveyor belts whatever was produced there,

and there was a blue-water harbour where it might be
transported along the coast, or to another coast.
We couldn't have told it from by-product or waste.
The soft rock fell to pieces in my hands.

To one side was a beach, with stones and trash.
Spongy sea-plants grew on it, and what looked like
bloodied thigh-bones but were only a different seaweed.
The sea spilt itself a little way on to the grey sand.

The Day After

I arrived on a warm day, early, a Sunday.
They were sweeping the gravel dunts of boules,
clearing away the wire rig and char of fireworks.
The red metal ornamental maples, planed and spinning
like globes on stalks, had caught the sun.

The cups of the fountains were running over.
A few drops rolled back on the underside, trailed along,
tense and brimming, and fell into the common pool
like ships going over the edge of the world:
the roaring waters, the stolid, day-long rainbow . . .

It struck eight, nine. There was no wind
to blow the glassy fountains off course. My eyes hurt
from the silver bedding plants and vermilion flowers.
I could almost believe the smooth, slabbed plinth
that said: They will rise again.

From A to B and Back Again

The Northern Line had come out into the open,
was leaving tracks like a curving cicatrice.
There was Barnet, my glottal stop, trying hard
to live up to its name, colloquial and harmless and trite.

The place was sunny and congested, brick and green trim,
it had the one-of-everything-and-two-butchers
of a provincial town. First, I dropped into
the maternity hospital by accident . . .

The porter was an analphabete, but together
we found your name, down among the Os,
and there you were, my brave love,
in a loose hospital gown that covered nothing;

pale; on an empty drip; and eager to show me
your scars, a couple of tidy crosses
like grappling hooks, one in the metropolis,
the other some distance away, in the unconcerned suburbs.

Days of 1987

I was lying out on the caesium lawn,
on the ribs and ligatures of a split deckchair,
under the Roman purple of a copper beech,
a misgrown fasces, all rods and no axe.

It was the double-zero summer, where the birds
stunned themselves on the picture windows
with no red bird cardboard cut-out doubles to warn them,
where the puffball dandelion grew twice as high,

where it was better not to eat parsley.
Every Friday, the newspapers gave fresh readings,
and put Turkish hazelnuts on the index.
A becquerel might be a fish or a type of mushroom.

In Munich, cylindrical missile balloons
bounced table-high, head-high, caber-high, house-high.
The crowds on the Leopoldstrasse were thick as pebbles
on the beach. I lay out on the caesium lawn.

Pastorale

FOR BEAT STERCHI

Where the cars razored past on the blue highway,
I walked, unreasonably, *contre-sens*,

the slewed census-taker on the green verge,
noting a hedgehog's defensive needle-spill,

the bullet-copper and bullet-steel of pheasants,
henna ferns and a six-pack of Feminax,

indecipherable cans and the cursive snout and tail
of a flattened rat under the floribund ivy,

the farmer's stockpiled hayrolls and his flocks,
ancillary, bacillary blocks of anthrax.

On the Beach at Thorpeness

I looked idly right for corpses in the underbrush,
then left, to check that Sizewell was still there.
The wind was from that quarter, northeasterly, a seawind,
B-wind, from that triune reliable fissile block.

—It blackened the drainage ditches
on the low coastal plain, blew up a dry tushing rustle
from the liberal-democratic Aesopian bullrushes,
and an ill-tempered creaking from Christian oaks . . .

A set of three-point lion prints padded up the beach.
The tideline was a ravel of seaweed and detritus,
a red ragged square of John Bull plastic,
a gull's feather lying down by a fish-spine.

The North Sea was a yeasty, sudsy brown slop.
My feet jingled on the sloping gravel,
a crisp musical shingle. My tracks were oval holes
like whole notes or snowshoes or Dover soles.

Roaring waves of fighters headed back to Bentwaters.
The tide advanced in blunt cod's-head curves,
ebbed through the chattering teeth of the pebbles.
Jaw jaw. War war.

Postcard from Cuernavaca

TO RALPH MANHEIM

Picture me
sitting between the flying buttresses of Cuernavaca Cathedral
reading Lawrence on the clitoral orgasm, and (more!)
his notion of replacing the Virgin Mary,
the one enduringly popular foreigner,
with Cortez' translator, later mistress, la Malinche,
the one enduringly unpopular—because xenophile—
    Mexican . . .

The night wind
blows the clouds over from the direction of his old palace,
a rather gloomy, conglomerate affair, pirated from an
    old pyramid,
and studded with red volcanic tufa in heart-sized pieces.
It's an even-handed museum now: offensively large statue
    of Cortez—
revisionist Rivera mural. (Or you turn away from both,
and look to where the volcanoes used to be.)

Out in front,
there are forests of helium balloons glittering under the
    fresno trees

where sociable black grackles natter and scream.
Hawkers trailing by in profile like matadors, trailing—in one
    case a hawk.
A Mariachi trumpeter, wearing just his old pesos,
trilling drily into the gutter. Ostensible Aztecs
stitching their silver Roman-style tunics im *Schneidersitz*.

There's a band
hidden in Eiffel's unilluminated iron snowdrop bandstand—
bought by the Austrians here to cheer them up
when Maximilian left the scene—giving it some humpity.
The rondure and Prussian gleam of the horns—
I sit and listen in the *Café Viena*.
Anything north of here goes, and most things east.

My room is both.
A steel door, pasteboard panelling,
and so high it makes me dizzy.
The toilet paper dangles inquiringly from the window cross.
A light bulb's skull tumbles forlornly into the room.
Outside there is a chained monkey who bites. He lives,
as I do, on Coke and bananas, which he doesn't trouble to peel.

Las Casas

I leaned round the corner in a Gold Rush town—
fortunate, apprehensive and somewhat surprised to be there.
The wind was one hazard, and so were the ramps
and unevennesses on the pavements, and the streetsellers
with their montóns of oranges. The kerbs were high,
almost a foot, as though anticipating a flood or blizzard.
Everyone seemed to have come from somewhere else,
the gringos from Europe and North America, the Ladinos,
once, ditto, the Indians from their outlying villages.
Everyone was a source of money to everyone else.
Who had it: the pink- or blue-burned and -burnoused
Indians; the women, in their bosoms with their babies;
the kerchiefed figures bussed in on the back of camiones;
the ugly, leggy, insouciant foreign girls;
or the Ladinos, of whom the Indians said
they were begotten by a Ladina and a dog
by the side of the road, 'the Ladina helping' . . . ?
It was a raw town. The shoe shops sold mincing machines,
hats and aluminium buckets shared a shelf, paper and iron
went together—for the staking of claims, perhaps?
A town of radio shops and funeral parlours—
the dead travelled to the aquamarine graveyard
in station wagons, horizontal, to music;

the living, upright, on pickups, also to music.
Of well-lit drink shops. Of illustrated marriage magazines
and spot-the-beachball shots in Kodak shops.
Of *Secrets of a Nunnery*, and two churches
facing each other on two hills, holding a lofty dialogue.
(One was a ruin.) Of patio-and-parapet housing,
and pastel shacks whose quick spread swallowed the airport.
Of unpaved streets, away from the centre.
Of everyone off the streets, paved or not, by eight o'clock.
Of the all-day screech of tortilla machines
and the scrape of rockets up the sky, a flash in the pan,
a percussive crash, a surprisingly durable cloud.
Jubilation, and no eyes raised.

Progreso

The crazy zocalo tips at a loco angle.
It pours three hundred infant girls, dressed
like Christmas-tree fairies, down the church's throat, singing.
A thin trickle of demonstrators chant 'iMexico!' uphill.

Whitewashed against white ants, the yew tree trunks
look spindly and phosphorescent, like stalagmites
in the cavern of their shade. The birds won't sing.
An old man clutches a fistful of drumsticks and shivers.

A month after the election, the posters are still up,
each x-ing out counted as a vote for the winner,
the loser has lost his shirt and scowls like a prizefighter,
and the Party of the Institutionalised Revolution marches on.

Every shoe is a spurred boot, every hat is a stetson,
every car a Dodge pickup. In hat and boots, every man is seven
    feet tall,
twelve standing on his Dodge. On Coffinmaker Street,
a bottle goes from hand to hand, from the left hand to the right.

Sunday in Puebla

dies amara valde

I saw the same face
on the bloody Jerusalem Christ in Puebla Cathedral,
on the 'Martyr of the Revolution', Aquiles Serdán,
and the law student, Gumaro Amaro Ramírez.

The Christ lay coffined in glass like Lenin.
He had more than the usual five wounds,
he had all the abrasions and contusions consistent with being
    crucified.
—He must have been the work of a police artist.

In 1910, the police laid siege to Serdán's house
(now the Original Museum of the Mexican Revolution).
It was a slow night,
he hid under the floorboards for eighteen hours—

there was the neat trapdoor, out of *Doctor Faustus* or *Don Giovanni*—
and when he came up, crying 'Don't shoot!'
one bullet passed through his windpipe,
another unhinged the top of his head.

Gumaro had his life-sized picture
in a colour tabloid,

though his skin was white, and his blood almost black.
It was said the Governor had wanted him dead.

A dreadful indifference took me
in the room full of Mexican tricolors—
the same eagle on the same cactus chewing on the same worm—
and in the room of mildly heretical old banknotes,

the room with pious acrylic paintings of the siege by modern artists,
the room with photographs of the march-past of 1931,
and the one gallery with portraits of the Governors' of Puebla,
and the other with those of the Presidents of Mexico.

And later too,
where Christians packed the church
on the site where Cortez had sacrificed Aztecs
on their own altars—

Christians in sweatpants,
Christians rocking up in flexitime,
Christians leaping hotfoot from racing bicycles in long tight
    black shorts,
Christians carrying 40-watt Puerto Rican briefcases . . .

The sun shone all that day as it did most days,
the young Mexicans were visibly fond of one another,
and red spiky chrysanthemum blossoms were starting to appear
on the otherwise bare colorín trees.

Aerogrammes, 1–5

It felt like my life talking to me—after two months,
talking to me again—saying it had bought a new duvet
but was still dithering on the matter of children,
that it had been seeing a lot of its friends—it wondered
whether it was truly in love with me—and had enjoyed
some pleasantly successful moments at work, but it wasn't
eating or sleeping properly, and was talking far too much.

Guanajuato Two Times

FOR KARL MILLER

A smiling woman in a rebozo holding up a rebozo . . .
—SYBILLE BEDFORD

I could keep returning to the same few places
till I turned blue; till I turned into
José José
on the sleeve of his new record album,
'What Is Love?';
wearing a pleasant frown and predistressed denims;
reading the double-page spread ('The Trouble with José José')
on his drink problem,
comparing his picture 'Before' and 'After' . . .
I could slowly become a ghost, slowly familiar,
slowly invisible, amiable, obtuse . . .
I could say 'Remember me?' to the blank bellhop,
and myself remember
the septet in the bandstand playing 'Winchester Cathedral',
and the clown coming in for coffee
and to count his takings and take off his face . . .
I could take on all my former beds for size.
Meander knowingly through twelve towns with twelve street
    names between them.

Sit on both sides of the municipal kissing seats,
shaking my head at the blanket men
and the hammock men, in their humorous desperation
offering me hammocks for four, for five, for six . . .
I could learn the Spanish for
'I shall have returned' or 'Hullo, it's me again!'
and get the hang of the double handshake,
first the palms, then the locked thumbs.
My dreams would moulder and swell and hang off me
like pawpaws. I could stand and sway like a palm,
or rooted like a campanile, crumbling slightly
each time the bells tolled, not real bells
but recordings of former bells,
and never for me.

APPROXIMATELY NOWHERE

(1999)

For Gert Hofmann, died 1 July 1993

The window atilt, the blinds at half-mast,
the straw star swinging in the draught, and my father
for once not at his post, not in the penumbra
frowning up from his manuscript at the world.

Water comes running to the kitchen to separate
the lettuce for supper from the greenflies who lived there.
The sill clock ticks from its quartz heart, the everlasting radio
has its antenna bent where it pinked his eye once.

Ink, tincture of bees, the chair for him,
the chair for my mother, the white wastepaper basket
empty and abraded by so much balled-up paper,
nosebleeds and peach-pits.

The same books as for years, the only additions by himself,
an African mask over the door to keep out evil spirits,
a seventeenth-century genre scene—the children
little adults—varnished almost to blackness.

Outside, the onetime pond packed with nettles,
the cut-down-we-stand of bamboo, the berries
on the mountain ash already orange and reddening, although
the inscrutable blackbirds will scorn them months more.

What Happens

Blood heat at the place of the bleeding, base
of the skull, a new scowling set to my mouth,
scattiness, contempt, emulousness, laughter,
the hysterical use of the present tense.

Directions

The new   south east cemetery
is approximately   nowhere
ten stops by underground   then bus
zigzagging   through the suburbs
as bad as Dachau   and you end up
still getting out   a stop early
at the old   south east cemetery
on which it abuts   tenements
market gardens expressways   and then
it's huge   carp in the ponds gardeners
drunks rolling on the paths   fighting
lavender and roses   round the corner
is a café   with an upstairs
long long tables   and slabs of cake

Last Walk

The two of you, thirty-seven years married,
and only to one another, I should add—

some odd stone or metal for that, or medal—
arm in arm, old, stable (your new trick,

except at your age you don't learn new tricks,
more as if all your lives you'd understudied

age and stability), me buzzing round you
like an electron, first one side then the other,

the long walk by the concrete-bedded river,
the Sempt, whose tributaries arrive in pipes,

the heavy July whiff of river and linden,
low water, weeds, a few fish,

the ducks beside themselves at nightfall,
the unfailingly noisy dog and cherished for it,

the last remaining farm in the new suburb,
alteingesessen, a hayfield among garden plots,

all the way up to the quarry pool,
the gigantic activity of the new airport

racing day and night to completion like a new book,
and somewhere in it all, your tenderness

for a firefly.

Endstation, Erding

And the walk the other way, right out of the front door,
hat and wife and dark glasses—never now wifeless—
to shop in Kaiser's general store in the *lange Zeile*

(*calle, ulice*) with the battered, supposedly
indestructible maroon and yellow nylon shoulder bag,
a kind of compendious ribbon, a hand-held trawl net . . .

Shopping, like most everything, the opposite
of what it was once, economies now, bargains,
a rough and ready diet for high blood and diabetes,

but he took the same pleasure in it, bruised bananas,
knocked down but *tadellos* inside, weathered bread,
and still the old ungovernable flair for luxury,

weisst du noch, Krimsekt. Always happy shopping,
something in prospect, something to talk about,
a rest from the silvered goldfishbowl of consciousness . . .

The walk through the deserted postmodern forum
of cobbles and fountains, past the credit-happy bank,
the jink through the local newspaper office,

the library after a week taking down its display of novels
and its card *In Gedenken an Gert Hofmann* †,
the railway signals still up with the line long gone.

Zirbelstrasse

FOR MY MOTHER, AND IN MEMORY OF MY FATHER

She's moving out of the house now, the sticky sycamores
one after the other struck by lightning outside the picture
    window
that my father struck by lightning liked to keep curtained
before the lightning came for him a second time early one
    morning
and he lost his balance, his speech, and last of all his mischief,

the high pines that gave the street its name chopped down
by the new people, only the birches left standing
whose thin leaves and catkins reminded me of her copper
    silver hair,
the old woman upstairs with all her marbles and mobility
put in a home by her Regan of a daughter who sold the house

over the heads of my parents, sitting-duck tenants,
bourgeois gypsies, wheeled suitcases on top of fitted wardrobes,
the windows where my sister's criminal boyfriends climbed in
    at night,
over the hedge the pool where the dentist's children screamed,
the old couple next door, *Duzfreunde* of Franz Josef Strauss,

the patio stones with their ineradicable growths of moss,
the weedy lawn where slugs set sail of an evening and met
   their ends
like Magellan, sliced up in the salty shallows of their own froth,
the potatoes my father bestirred himself to grow one year,
gravelly bullets too diamond hard to take a fork,

moving with all the books, the doubtful assets of a lifetime,
the steel table only I had the wit to assemble and left my feet on,
the furniture and lamps picked up in border raids to Italy,
once austerely challenging, now out-of-date moderne,
too gloomy to read by, and sad as anything not bought old,

the Strindberg kitchen with the dribbling Yugoslav fridge,
the Meissen collection we disliked and weren't allowed to use,
the démodé gadgets for making yoghurt, for Turkish coffee,
the turkey cutlets not so much cooked as made safe in the
   frying pan,
the more cooking cut corners and dwindled and became rehash,

my off-and-on kingdom in the cellar, among the skis and old boots,
my father's author's copies and foreign editions,
the blastproof metal doors, preserves, tin cans and board-games
of people who couldn't forget the Russians, the furnace room
where my jeans were baked hard against an early departure.

Still Life

A sort of overgrown phial,
opaque blown glass of the sort
we once saw them making at Murano,
whitish—with blue? with yellow?

And sticking out of it
that odd trouvaille, a dried yard
of was it hogweed, *Schweinekraut*,
Schweinswurzel, something swinish about it,

some hollow dill-like plant
withered to articulate straw
that my father half-inched,
like a spindly triffid on the steel table.

It was an artistic endeavour really,
a momentary juxtaposition
that gathered dust, languishing
like umbrella ribs in an elephant's foot,

in *saecula saeculorum*.
As it grew dark, he drew the curtains,
so as not to be seen, or not to show
how much he couldn't see.

There was a drawn atmosphere
as in Buñuel or *La Grande Bouffe*,
like being locked up overnight
in an impoverished modern art museum

—as it were, Beuys in Buffalo—

and we slumped like astronauts
in the too-low leather seats
while he peeled and chopped fruit
and handed it around.

de passage

From you I know we owe it to the others
to make more of an effort,

to talk to the stallholders
in something approaching their language,

to pass the time of day—all that regular guy,
homme du peuple stuff that so dismayed me—

to stand in gatherings feet crossed
like apprehensive flamingoes,

to issue oblique challenges
to senior colleagues with a shy smile,

and not to go abroad in the garden suburbs
we've temporarily lucked into

without a pair of scissors in our pockets.

Cheltenham

The nouveau oil building
spoils the old water town, spook town, old folks' town.
My old parents, like something out of Le Carré,
shuffle round the double Georgian square

tracing figures of eight, endless figures of eight,
defected ice-dance trainers or frozen old spooks,
patinage, badinage,
reminiscence with silences.

Then a family event if ever there was one:
my mother reads my translation of my father,
who hasn't read aloud since his 'event'.
Darkness falls outside. Inside too.

Ted Hughes is in the small audience,
and afterwards asks my father
whether he ever, like an Inuit,
dreamed of his own defeat and death.

My father, who's heard some questions, but never anything
like this, doesn't know Ted Hughes,
perhaps hears 'idiot', gives an indignant no
in his miraculously clear English.

More laps of the marred green,
the pink sky silts down, a November afternoon
by the clock, his last in England.
The days brutally short; a grumpy early night.

Metempsychosis

Your race run, the rest of us,
mother, sisters, sisters' boyfriends,
ran repairs. Trimmed the hedge,
whited the walls, weeded the stones.

The place looked five years younger—
you might not have recognised it.
It took you dead to harness us,
give us some common, Tolstoyan purpose.

It was the day the ants queened themselves,
or whatever they do. Got to the end,
and came back all self-conscious with silver wings,
folding stuff they hardly knew what to do with.

Like the Ossis in Berlin, they got everywhere
(a run on cuckoo clocks). The clever ones
would go far, to be in position for
the next pedestrian incarnation.

Essex

FOR LAVINIA GREENLAW

They turned your pet field into a country club,
and the cemetery was grey with rabbits
and the graves of your friends
who had died young, of boredom.

Fidelity

FOR JAMES, AGAIN

At the old *Tramontana*
on Tottenham Court Road
among the hi-fi shops
I learned to order

what you ordered,
not studenty noodles
but sophisticated things
like the special.

After years of our
playing at lunch,
the old waiter shook himself
to death with Parkinson's

practically before our eyes.
(I remember the rattle
and slop of one last
saucerful of coffee.)

One afternoon,
when we no longer went there

like Hem to the War,
I saw Joseph Brodsky

sitting in the window
with paper and a cigarette,
the recording angel,
miles away.

Ingerlund

The fat boy by Buddha out of Boadicea
with the pebbledash acne and half-timbered haircut,
sitting on the pavement with his boots in the gutter,

we must have made his day when we pulled over
and asked him for the site of the Iron Age fort
in his conservation village.

Parerga

In the bedside drawer of a hotel room
in the black-naugahyde-and-pigtail German Eighties,
I came upon the Yellow Pages and a Gideon Bible,
one of them—which one?—
pregnant with the local chickenhawk guide.

Vecchi Versi

It's just abstract, you say: when I'm not here,
I don't exist and my perspectives are warped.
Nostalgia, the bloom of recollection—
a false spring . . . You can't run your life
by these conceits like productivity agreements.

. . . It's a holiday of some sort.
The music on the radio is for kissing.
You go to visit your thin-lipped friend,
who happens to be a musician himself.

You drink wine and sit at a table
and talk. Some things you talk around.
Then you are on the same side of the table.
He has some Durex, you let him fuck you.
—He was kind of lonesome, as the words go.

(1980)

131

Intimations of Immortality

Have a nice day and get one free—
this is retirement country,
where little old ladies

squinny over their dashboards
and bimble into the millennium,
with cryogenics to follow;

the shuttle astronauts
hope to fluff re-entry and steal
one last record-breaking orbit;

where they give a man
five death sentences
to run more or less concurrently.

I take turns in my three chairs,
and try to remember two switches for lights,
the third for waste.

My eyes sting from salt and sun-oil,
and I drink orange juice
till it fizzes and after.

The sight of a cardinal
or the English Sundays on Thursday
makes it a red letter day.

Lizards flirt in the swordgrass,
grasshoppers bow their thighs
at six sharp, and quite suddenly,

after seventy-five years,
the laurel oak crashes out.
See you later, if not before.

(GAINESVILLE)

Rimbaud on the Hudson

Some kill somewhere upstate. Bud light,
a gutted mill, three storeys of brickwork,
mattresses and condoms, elder and sumac,
child abusers fishing for chub in heavy water.

Scylla and Minos

I knew about Helen, they kept selling me Helen,
but I never even got to be stolen in the first place.
Sieges are boring—did you know. Everything's fine,
just each day's a little bit worse than the last.

And you start thinking how long it is since you saw
prawns or a nice pair of earrings or a magazine.
I had my townhouse, but I practically lived on the battlements,
they even let me use the telescope during the lulls.

Then one day I saw him. That changed everything.
Oiled limbs, greaves (can you imagine), his little skirt,
roaring and rampaging about, the bellowed (yes, taurean)
    commands.
By Jupiter out of Europa, apparently. I thought: gimme!

A big girl wants a man like that, not the little weasels
scurrying around defending me. (Did I ask to be defended?)
I started cheering him on as he skewered our guys.
I wondered if he could see me and what he thought.

Was he stuffing a goat, hitting the 3 star, or letters home?
Minos, Minos King of Crete. I tried on a Cretan accent,
did that all the hair up all the hair down thing they do there.
I thought of the word Argive—or were we the Argives?

Perhaps if we lost—and how could we fail to lose,
how could anyone hold out against him, he's so irresistible—
then I'd get to be his wife or his sex slave or something.
Who cares, frankly. Isn't that what happens. After a war?

That's when I started thinking about trying to help things along.
Not pushing 'our boys' over the edge, or distracting them from
    the job in hand
by giving them blow jobs as they manned the walls (man
    something else),
something more ruthless, I suppose, and more wholesale.

I wrote to Minos, signed 'a fan', to meet me at the gate.
It wasn't easy, believe me. At night I spiked their drinks.
I went into Daddy's bedroom with the garden shears
and cut off his purple scalplock. The creepy thing went and
    bled on me.

There. I shouldn't have told you. Anyway, I popped it in a bag
and ran to the Maidens' Gate. He wasn't there, of course.
So I had to pick my way through his dreaming army
with it in my hands, by now it was hissing softly.

He was up, of course (so conscientious!),
in something skimpy, bustling about his tent,
wet jockstraps hanging up to dry. (What I'd give!)
The funny thing is he didn't seem pleased to see me, I looked.

I said: This is the purple hair of Nisus.
The siege is over. Invest the town. (Invest me!)
He got all huffy, gave me stuff about war and men and honour,
said something so underhand had no place in the annals, etc.,

and no way was I ever going to Crete at his side.
I said did he like war so much, he didn't want it to end.
The next day his flag was flying over Megara
and they were loading the ships.

He dictated peace terms. My father abdicated.
I stumbled about the campsite, thinking what I'd done,
what there was for me to do. I couldn't go back,
and which of the other towns on the strip would have me—

like giving houseroom to the Trojan horse,
the Trojan bicycle more like. It was Crete or nothing.
He stood by the mast, arms crossed, for all the world like Ulysses.
I said: Fuck you, Minos, your wife does it with bulls!

Then I saw my father coming for me, he was an osprey,
he was rejuvenated, I gave a little mew of terror,
and found myself flying too, criss-crossing the sea,
Scylla the scissor-legged, now the shearer.

Gone

FOR JAMIE McKENDRICK

The usual roses on the dado, the curtain, the bedspread
and the oriental picture with cranes,
clashing with the usual magnolia on the walls . . .

The television swings into the room on a hinged extension
like a box camera or a boxing glove
or something at the dentist's.

The radio and Teasmaid are perched on shooting sticks,
the two-handled diamanté neon bedside lamp
is an apple of discord—all mine!

An hour's sleep on the back of eight hours of drink.
From the street comes the *beep beep* of Green Goddesses reversing.
Two suns appear in the mitred window.

Vagary

I can really only feign disapproval
of my youngest
dibbling his semolina'd fingers
in the satiny lining of her red coat.

June

Did we really open with 'Sweetness'?
—LLOYD COLE, liner notes

Short forms. Lines, sentences, *bonmots*.
Part of an afternoon, a truncated night,
interstitial evening. Rarely a paragraph
or stanza ('room'), never a day and a day and a day . . .
Half-pints and double-deckers, the river, the cemetery,
always on the *qui vive* (why, ourselves of course!)—
our honeymoon epic in illicit instalments.

Megrim

Corners of the linden yellow like grapes . . .
back in July leaves blew. Rain wounds the window,
preoccupies the drainpipes, nourishes—
after a seemly interval—the mould spots
in the cornices. Stray nooses of wisteria
toss purposefully, aimlessly, who can say.

Near Hunstanton

These are my own crows in a mechanical flap;
my geese in ragged Vs—more Ws or Ys—
honking abysmally to one another;

my salt marsh smelling of vomit
at low tide, grown with tiny plants
the colour of rust; my oak leaves

imitating rain with their eczematic rustle;
my stone-scabbed beach impounded
peu à peu by the sea; my soft low cliffs

crumbling their beach-huts to the Northeaster;
my big skies you can see coming a mile away;
my jellyfish that you trod on in your sensible shoes.

Seele im Raum

I could probably
just about have swung a cat
in that glory-hole—

maybe a Manx cat
or that Cheshire's gappy grin—
and for a fact I could open the door

and perhaps even the window
without raising myself
off the plumbed-in sofa

but what really hurt
was the rugby football
deflating from lack of use,

a pair of void calendars
and the pattern of my evenings
alone on the slope

overlooking the playground
the paddling pool
gradually drained of children

the bullying park attendant
crows sipping from beer cans
as if they'd read Aesop,

sun gone, a nip in the air,
the grass purpling
and cold to the touch,

and later on, in near darkness,
watching a man's two boomerangs
materialise behind him

out of the gloom,
like the corners of his coffin
on leading-strings.

XXXX

FOR LARRY JOSEPH

que lo único que hace es componerse
de dias;
que es lóbrego mamífero y se peina . . .
—VALLEJO

I piss in bottles,
collect cigarette ash in the hollow of my hand,
throw the ends out of the window
or douse them in the sink.

I chew longlife food,
dried fruit, pumpernickel, beef jerky.
I'm forty. I free the jammed light-push with my fingernails
to give the hall a rest.

With one stockinged foot—scrupulous pedantry—
I nudge back the loose stair-carpet on the eleventh step.
Later I might slam some doors
and spend a wet evening under a tree.

I've identified with a yellowish fox beside the railway line,
followed silent firework displays on the Thames,
seen two shooting stars burn out over London
and made wishes on them.

I can't remember when I last wrote a letter
or picked up the telephone. My smile
goes on shopkeepers and bus drivers and young mothers.
It dazzles me.

I think continually about money, and the moths eat my clothes:
the thing about earthly treasures was true.
For half an hour, amid palpitations, I watched
two children I was sure were mine.

Most of the day I'm either lying down
or asleep. I haven't read this many books
this avidly since I was a boy.
Nights are difficult. Sometimes I shout.

I'm quarrelsome, charming, lustful, inconsolable, broken.
I have the radio on as much as ever my father did,
carrying it with me from room to room.
I like its level talk.

Malvern Road

It's only a short walk, and we'll never make it,
the street where we first set up house—
set up maisonette—together ... do you remember
the grim Tuesday *Guardian* Society-section aspect of it,
the crumbly terrace on one side,
then the road, modern and daunting but somehow in truce,

and the high-rises and multi-storey garages opposite
that gave us our view, and in winter,
like a periscope five miles away due south,
the GPO tower obliterated by Paddington Rec the rest of the time,
and that was the only way to go from where we were,
'barely perched on the outer rim of the hub of decency',

probably we were happy but in any case
we were beyond dreams in the strange actualness of everything,
a tyro salary, a baby mortgage, such heartstopping fun,
the place too intimate and new and connected to us
for us to think of 'entertaining'
and we liked the stairs best of everything anyway,

the *ancien* lino kitchen
where I cooked out of *The Pauper's Cookbook*

—'a wealth, or should it be, a poverty of recipes'—
the bedroom barely wide enough to take our bed crosswise,
so we lay next to the window, the window making a third,
the creased cardboard blind bleaching like jeans,

everything cheap and cheerful,
your jaunty primary touches everywhere, fauve and mingled,
my room a grave navy ('Trafalgar') with my vast desk
like an aircraft carrier that I had to saw the legs off
to get upstairs, and then fitted the stumps on casters
so when I wrote it rolled,

the muso downstairs and on the ground floor
the night cook with the farouche squint,
his placid Spanish wife and their little Sahara,
how frightening everything was,
and with how much faith, effort and heart
we went out to meet it anyway,

the corner pub we probably never set foot in,
the health centre padlocked and grilled like an offie,
the prefab post office set down at an odd angle,
the bank that closed down, the undertaker who stayed open,
the idealistic delicatessen before God and Thatcher created
    the zuppie,
the tremulous restaurant my best friend proposed in,

the sun breeding life from dirt like Camus,
the pepper-fruited scrawny alder with two yellow days of pollen,
the nights of your recurring dream
where you whimpered comfort to your phantom baby boy
you didn't have and said you'd mind him, as now,
to my shame, you have and you do.

Lewis Hollow Road

The walls—sloping like a tent's—of pre-slathered plasterboard
depending from a single great beam, the slushy track outside a
    bobsleigh run
negotiated by the neighbours' four-wheel drives at odd hours,
the black metamorphic bulk of the treetrunk through the night,
icicles dripping and growing and shrinking and forking like
    Tirpitz's beard,

the outside in in the form of quills and feathers and stingray
    bones and pine cones,
Indian burial chamber bric-a-brac, the six-foot rattler in the
    mudroom,
a Spanish guitar and a Dustbuster hanging together like a
    yellow-grey Braque,
the alphabetical books at rest on many shelves and the
    unsleeping regard
of Auden and Burroughs on postcards, the sacred monsters of
    the place,

gods of incompatible religions, ourselves under a couple of
    blankets,
one of them notionally electric, sometimes knotted together in
    brief sleep,

as often each hugging his edge of the bed, lying three or four
    bodies apart,
wrestling with ourselves and our doubts and miseries, and
    you asking,
awkwardly, unexpectedly, apropos of nothing much: 'Do you
    think I'm real?'

Fairy Tale

and smoke too many cigarettes
and love you so much
—FRANK O'HARA

It was blowing hot and cold as I sat in the window seat
in a northern town, the heating on in June,
the window sash propped open on a splint of wood
like a tired eye on a matchstick . . .

There was a sign, *Thank you for not smoking*,
but I didn't want thanks, I wanted to smoke.
I was living on air, cigarettes, pull-ups and kisses—
puffing away in a daze of longing.

Outside was the delicate viaduct, a redoubt,
a pair of magpies mating. The sun shone,
and there was such a fine rain falling,
no rainbow was required.

It struck me I was exactly the person
to write the life of the pink shopping bag
hovering irresolutely
on the triangular intersection below.

It's puzzling how things happen. For years,
the princess lies in the glass coffin of her life,
then fruit on her tongue, and beer,
and salt, your salt.

Gomorrah

e l'inferno è certo. —MONTALE

The queer cemetery
torsos jacent on tombstones
old-fashioned looks

no conversation
not about muscles
or gyms or tans

as comforting
in its blithe transgressiveness
as a stolen baked potato

and you and I
hand in hand
looking for shade

and an untenanted
patch of grass
close to the railway line

with the new stand
at Stamford Bridge
going up behind us

or again
on top of the hill at night
in the killing heat

kein Lüftchen weht
the view of Canary Wharf
and a fizzy orange-purple sky

and at our feet the park police van
tracking an athlete
round the cinder track

surrounded by a heavenly host
twitting and outwith
guarding our guardians.

Night Train

In the half-compartment
set aside for the handicapped
I crossed my feet on the battered
fire-extinguisher,

the grandfather, maybe,
of my shaken can of County
foaming at the widget,

and sat remembering the dowdily
glaring train back from Guildford,
feeling parched and let down
after our reading,

the series of benighted stops
where no one got on
—much less got off—

at one of which, at least,
I put it to you, not joking,
though you weren't to know that then,
that we might elope together

somewhere in Wild West Surrey,
wo sich die Füchse gute Nacht sagen,
before we could reach

Suburbiton and Esher
Welcomes Careful Drivers,
the sporting meccas
of Wimbledon and Twickers,

the windows of the jolly poly
where you worked behind the bar
in a thriftstore bronze dress

and short back and sides,
chronically undecided
between Venus Pandemos
and Jeanne d'Arc.

Litany

FOR ROBIN ROBERTSON

Dear god,
        let me remember these months of transition
in a room on the Harrow Road, the traffic
muffled by a plastic sheet, the facing ziggurats
with their satellite dishes and tea-towels out to dry,
a lengthwise Brazilian flag curtaining one window,

indigents and fellow aliens and oddballs in the street,
the wobbly eyes I mistakenly looked into, wobbly and then
suddenly murderous, the fat friendly ladies and truanting children,
West Indian barbers and Lebanese grocers eating on the job,
the line of a hundred people outside the post office
at a minute to nine on Monday morning,

the pallet, table and two chairs
in the room at the top of the sharp and loose coir staircase,
a kettle and ashtray before I remembered about food,
the streetlamp almost within reach to slide down, fireman-style,
im *Falle eines Falles*,
the reflections of car windscreens bouncing on the ceiling,

the solicitous Irish landlady, Marie's sister, saying
'Are you alright? Now are you sure you're alright?'

the canal at the back, seedy as Xochimilco,
the May air full of seeds, alder and plane and sycamore,
generative fluff, myself fluffy and generative,
wild-haired and with the taste of L. in my mouth,

the office workers opposite
very evidently pissing behind milk-glass,
goslings and baby coots without the white stripe as yet,
attack dogs defecating on the grass,
the occasional putter of narrow boats, industrial
and bucolic as canals are industrial and bucolic,

the velvet curtains slowly turning to dust on the woodwormed rail,
my diminished establishment of bin-liners and suitcase
(our 1961 cardboard family 'Revelation'),
the Olympia Traveller I lugged around Mexico and two pairs
    of boots,
otherwise silence and light and dust and flies,
so hungry I picked the bin when I visited my children,

the steel doors and squats of Walterton and Elgin
from the days before pastel paint, a hulking unmistakable school
on the light industrial skyline, barbed wire, coupling pigeons,
yellow brick and corrugated Homebase prefab, living for nightfall
and the bus that took me round the houses
to heaven.

NEW POEMS

Motet

It's naphtha now you're gone
a sudden apprehension of squalor
the unflowering cardamom plant
gummy with syrup and flies
sour footsmell in the rumpled quilt
a wilted squadron of paper airplanes
ready to take me after you.

Broken Nights

FOR BILL AND MARY GASS

Then morning comes,
saying, 'This was a night.'
—ROBERT LOWELL

Broken knights.
—No, not like that.
Well, no matter.
Something agreeably
Tennysonian (is there
Any other kind?)
About 'broken knights'.
Sir Bors and Sir Bedivere.
In my one-piece pyjamas—
My it-doesn't-matter suit,
With necessarily non-matching
—Matchless, makeless, *makeles*—
Added top, I pad
Downstairs to look
At the green time
On the digital microwave.
My watch, you must know,
Died on my watch

All at the top, at midnight,
After a few
Anguished weeks of macro-
biotic stakhanovite
5-second ticks,
And I haven't had
Time, it seems,
To get it repaired.
Further (weewee hours),
To patronise
My #2 bathroom *en bas*
(Though N.B.
Only for a pee).
Groping for a piss,
As the poet saith.
Wondering how soon
It might be safe
To turn on the wireless,
Without it being either
New Age
Help you through the night
Seducer mellotrons
(What's a tron, mellow I can do?)
Or merely
Dependency inducing

And *wehrzersetzend*,
Deleterious for morale of the troops.
I eat to the beat,
Then snooze to the news.
Drift off to *Morning Edition*.
Arise/Decline, Sir
Baa Bedwards.

Hudson Ride

ich weiss nicht, was soll es bedeuten —HEINE

Red and yellow bittersweet; Poughkeepsie;
the ice jags are silver, rush spikes gold
in the blue December. A big old eagle,

white head, white feet, perches on a tree
like a postage stamp or a glorified house cat.
Socks in *excelsis*.—God, what is it with separation?

A soft freeze. The woods are rusty stone, henna fuzz ravines,
snow slicks. Ice blinds and dries. Dazzles and steams.
Swans outside Croton. I sit in the train,

at the very back of the last car,
rueing every mile. Some sort of folly and exhilaration.
A caffeinated feeling of being all heart.

'Shouldn't I ask to hold to you forever'. I rather think I did ask.
They thought it was the New Rhine, here, or wanted to.
Rhinebeck. Germantown. Dutchess County.

My girl, someone's girl, her own girl. Perhaps
the only other time in my life I've opposed the machinery
and scale of the world. My personal insurrection.

Auflehnung. A leaning up against—say, and by preference,
you in your kitchenette and sweater among the hi-hats
and bolt-cutters and beheaded pin sculptures.

Now here come the hard options: the cracked old Nabisco plant,
West Point, Indian Point, Ossining, Rockland Psych.,
Drachenfels. Bacharach. Loreley. Loreley. Loreley.

Idyll

The windows will reflect harder, blacker, than before,
and fresh cracks will appear in the yellow brick.

There is no milkman or paper boy, but presumably
the lurid pizza flyers and brassy offers of loans

will continue to drop through the letter box.
The utilities will be turned off one by one,

as the standing orders keel over or lose their address,
though there was never that much cooking or bathing or

phoning went on here anyway—the fridge will stop its buzz,
the boiler its spontaneous combusting—till there is nothing

but a mustiness of gas. The dust will coil and thicken
ultimately to hawsers around pipes and wires;

ever more elaborate spiders' webs will sheet off the corners;
rust stains and mildew and rot will spread chromatically

below the holes in the roof, radiate from the radiators;
eventually mosses and small grasses and even admirable

wild flowers, hell, an elder or buddleia, push their heads
through the chinks between the boards; a useless volume
    of books—

who could ever read that many—will keep the moths entertained,
generations of industrious woodlice and silverfish

will leave their corpses on the clarty work-surfaces,
and a pigeon or two will hook its feet over the tarnished sink

and brood vacantly on its queenly pink toes.

Poem

When all's said and done, there's still
the joyful turning towards you
that feels like the oldest, warmest, and quite possibly
best thing in me that I must stifle,
almost as if you were dead,
or I.

End of the Pier Show

It was—what?—
the triumph of hope
over experience.
But what triumph
(and what hope)?

The continued display
of a kind of unreasonable
fortitude, the man—
Beowulf—stooping
to pick his severed head

off the sawdust, and doing it
again and again.
And she, the woman,
sold, to her mind,
on love

as a kind of motor syrup—
a green linctus—
that was slowly replacing
her blood.
Perhaps lycanthropy.

A pessimistic sublime.
They had made
their bed and they
were jolly well
going to lie in it.

The woman's persistent
complaint that
it wasn't a life,
the man shrugging,
going away, battening down,

daring her to do worse,
if not her worst.
Siege conditions.
And she bringing out
in him strange abysms

of new behaviour.
Everything went
so peculiarly,
spectacularly skewed.
They were fascinated

by what they seemed
to have contained.
Unspoolings of truths.

Such dire sayings
of hers. Such vehemence

out of his mouth.
Just as well really
his doggish gloom
met her prickliness
halfway.

Attritional chafe,
chafe, bridle
and chafe, and, periodically
a grin and tears.
Her good will

expressed itself
in a strange persistence
of affection that he
not unreasonably supposed
would last forever.

(It wasn't to do with him,
was it?)
When it stopped,
he didn't believe it.
He didn't know what to do.

He went hunting around
for the trip switch
that had made this darkness,
this withdrawal.
(Alas, he was never much

of an electrician.)
What happened
to their lovely
puppet theatre,
their grand knockabout?

November

FOR JAMIE BUCHAN

Eine Krähe hackt der anderen [nicht] die Augen aus.
—GERMAN PROVERB(S)

Crows on oaks and cranes and cooling towers,
the sky cracking up, and crows investigating
the cream of whatever crust cracks yellow, milling
early birds, Styrofoam beaker of coffee,
refill, refill, and a spot of red-eye gravy.

(LEAVING BONN)